*Dedicated to all the children
who are "DIFFERENT"*

Jade Heard It All!

Copyright © 2020 by Jade Owens
Illustrations by Javone Williams

All rights reserved. No part of this publication may be reproduced, distributed, or transmitted in any form or by any means, including photocopying, recording, or other electronic or mechanical methods, without the prior written permission of the publisher, except in the case of brief quotations embodied in critical reviews and certain other noncommercial uses permitted by copyright law.

ISBN (paperback) 978-1-6748-4862-4

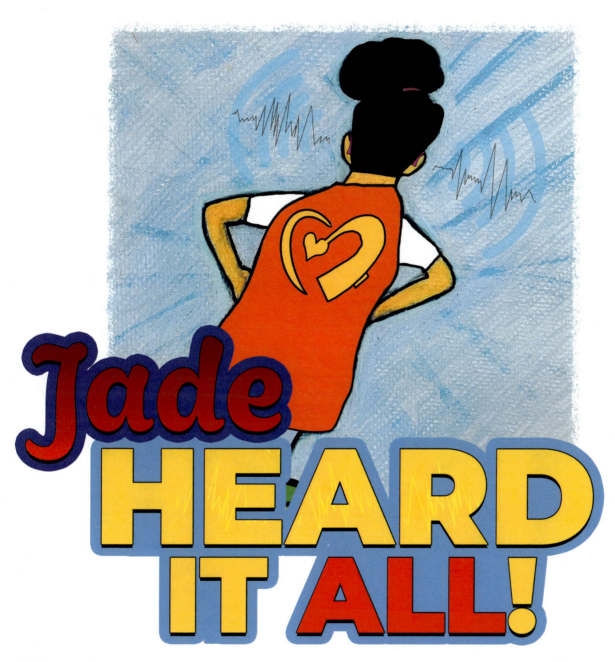

Written by
Jade Owens

Illustrated by
Javone Williams

My name is Jade Owens.

I am hearing impaired.

I have bilateral sensorineural hearing loss
which is why I wear hearing aids.

My hearing aids make learning easier and more fun.

This book is for all of the children who are just like me
and also children who aren't.

It's okay to be different!

Friends can look different, like different things,
and also have different needs.

I've learned we can all be friends
and learn new things from one another.

Jade Owens - Author

"USE YOUR LISTENING EARS" is always a rule all grown-ups teach kids.

And **ALL** kids know that means to be a great listener....

Well, not **ALL** kids have listening ears that work, no matter how hard they try.

I am **ONE** of those kids.

I have hearing loss.

I lost 50% of my hearing, so I wear a hearing aid to help me hear better.

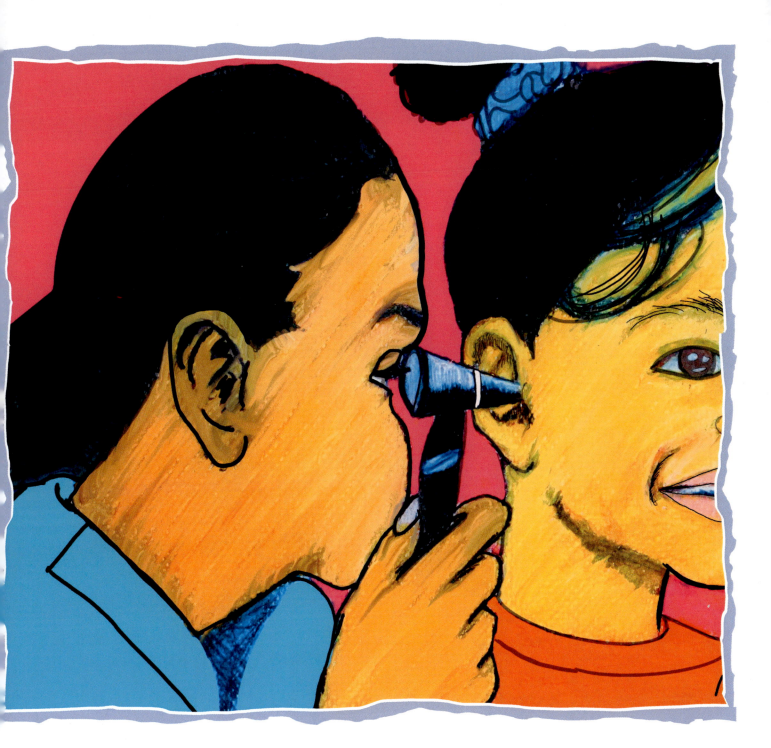

I can't even go swimming with them in my ears.

Oh GOSH, and the batteries die at the **WORST** time!

Lots of people stare at me when they notice my hearing aids....

And some even point
and laugh at me....

The teasing is the worst part
about wearing hearing aids.

It is **NOT** very kind.

But I don't let any of it get me down!

You want to know why?

That is what makes
having friends so cool.

Everyone is
DIFFERENT
in their own special way.

I AM PROUD OF MY HEARING AIDS.

They help me **HEAR** way better.

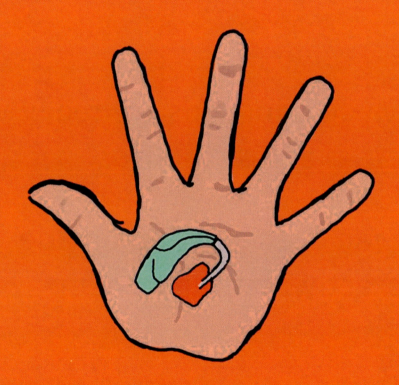

My hearing aids are really **cute** and **stylish!**

I can even get them made exactly how I like them.

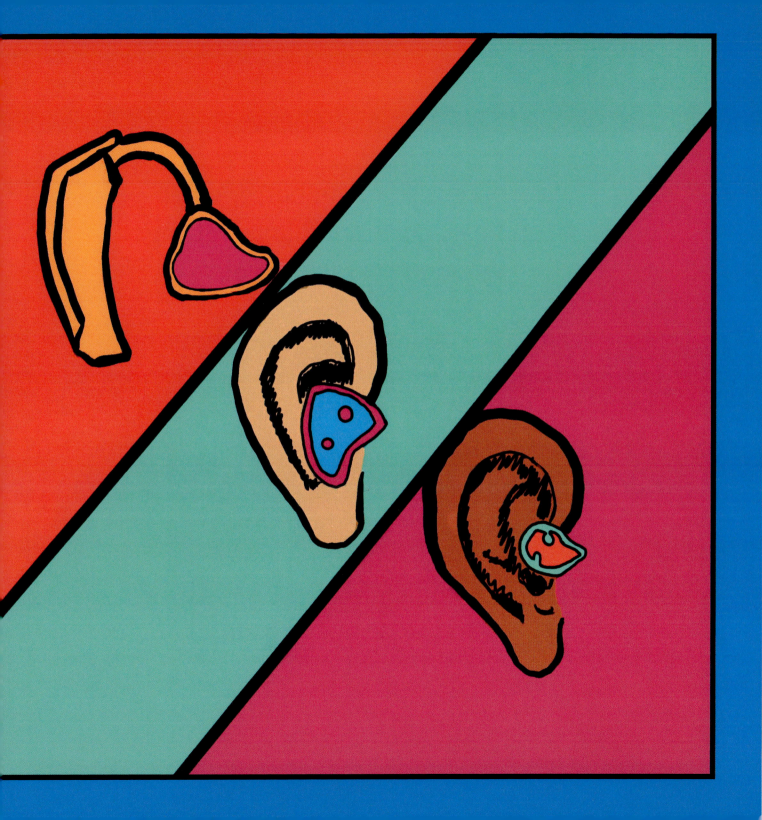

Learning is so much better when
I can hear more, and I love getting
good grades in school.

I also enjoy telling people all about my
hearing aids to help them understand.

I explain that I wear hearing aids to help me
hear and I am **BRAVE** enough to take them
out and show my friends!

It's like having a **super power**
when I wear hearing aids.

"I can hear it all."

It is like

MUSIC TO MY EARS.

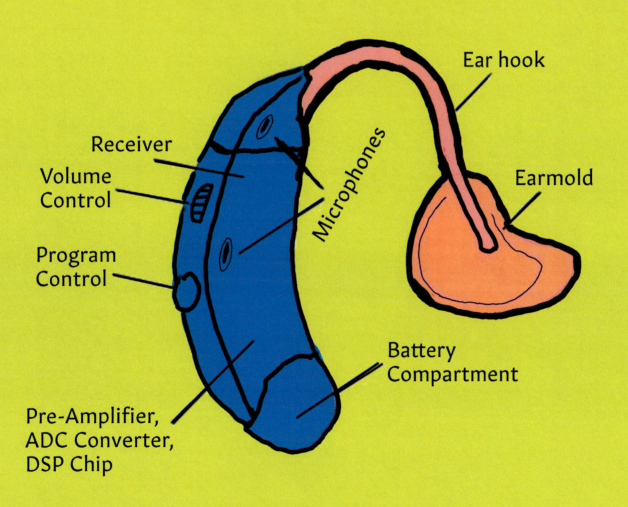

How would YOU design a HEARING AID?

Draw your own here:

I would like to thank my mommy for helping me write my book, my grandma Nikki for editing the book, Mr. Javone for drawing all of the cool pictures, GOD for making me special. Lastly, I want to thank my hearing aids because they are my best friends!

—**Jade Owens, Author**

www.jadehearditall.com
Instagram @jadehearditall

Made in the USA
Monee, IL
05 March 2021